What Children Reflect, What Adults Shape – As I See It

Verses Kindler Publication

Verses Kindler Publication.

Website: www.verseskindlerpublication.com

What Children Reflect, What Adults Shape – As I See It

By: Mrs. Antar Anger

ISBN: 978-93-47494-06-2

1st Edition

Price: INR 199/$11

Disclaimer

What Children Reflect, What Adults Shape – As I See It is authored by Antar Anger. The entirety of this published work comprises the original content of the author, who has undertaken diligent efforts in its editing. The characters depicted herein may be fictitious or inspired by real events; however, they are not intended to cause offense or represent any prejudice against any caste or system. Any similarity to the names of actual individuals, locations, or institutions is purely coincidental and serves the narrative. The author bears sole responsibility for the originality of this work; the publisher assumes no liability thereof.

Table of Contents

Chapter 1: The First Years: Early Childhood and Identity

It was a chilly morning as parents streamed into the sunny auditorium of Harmonia Ridge Academy, a liberal school located in the heart of the city. The occasion was a parent orientation for new students—an effort to create greater insight into the holistic philosophy of the school. Holding cups of coffee, some parents appeared apprehensive, others inquisitive, while a few were already familiar with one another from co-op groups or park gatherings. At the front of the room stood Ms. Lila Donovan, a child development specialist, prepared to offer more than mere information. She was inviting parents into an experience of rediscovery—of what it truly means to raise a conscious child in today's world.

"Good morning, everyone," she began, her voice soothing yet energetic. "Today, we're going to discuss something we often forget. It's about how early relationships shape not only what our children do, but who they believe they are." A quiet stir of interest moved through the room.

"We usually measure development through milestones—first words, first steps, the first day of school," she continued. "But beneath the surface, something much deeper is unfolding. A child's self-concept and social identity are being shaped moment by moment, primarily through their earliest interactions."

Lila paused and invited the parents to reflect more deeply. She explained that self-concept is the internal image a child forms of themselves—how they perceive their strengths, their worth, and their place in the world. This image does not arise in isolation. From birth, it develops through the mirror of others 'responses. When a baby laughs and is met with a warm smile, they learn, I am delightful. When a toddler's frustration is met with empathy, they learn, My feelings matter.

"At Harmonia Ridge," Lila added, "we also recognise that a child's sense of self emerges from their soul maturity—an innate awareness of who they are beyond this lifetime. Every child arrives with a unique energetic blueprint shaped by past experiences, soul purposes, and karmic lessons. Some children carry an old-soul wisdom, while others are here to explore entirely new ways of being."

The room grew quiet and reflective.

"This is where you, as caregivers, come in," she said gently. "Your emotional, psychological, and spiritual maturity can either support your child's journey of self-discovery or unintentionally hinder it. Caregivers are both mirrors and guides."

She explained that early peer relationships do not begin in playgrounds but within families—through parents, grandparents, siblings, and caregivers. These early bonds become the child's first mirrors, reflecting what is acceptable, lovable, or undesirable. If caregivers were taught to suppress emotions, they may unknowingly discourage emotional expression in their children. Unresolved shame or trauma can also be transmitted silently, through tone, behaviour, and emotional presence.

When one parent asked how to parent consciously despite having had a difficult childhood, Lila smiled. "Awareness is the beginning," she said. "When you commit to your own healing, your capacity to hold space for your child naturally expands. Parenting is not about perfection; it's about growing alongside your child."

She then introduced a deeper dimension, explaining that no child enters a family by chance. There are soul agreements and pre-birth contracts that bring children, parents, siblings, classmates, and even challenging teachers together for mutual growth. Growth, she reminded them, does not occur in isolation—it unfolds through relationships.

Lila described how karmic patterns may influence early behaviour. A child struggling to share may be unwinding patterns of scarcity, while another showing deep empathy may be healing past experiences of loss. When caregivers recognise this, they respond with compassion rather than judgment. "You may not always understand what your child is expressing," she said softly, "but you can always meet it with curiosity and love."

As children grow, she explained, peer interactions play an increasing role in shaping identity. Group play teaches cooperation, boundaries, and social roles. Children may begin to identify as "the funny one," "the helper," or "the leader" based on feedback they receive. These identities can either empower or restrict. Teachers at Harmonia Ridge are trained to notice such labels and gently guide children toward exploring their full range of being.

"Social identity is not limited to race, culture, or gender," Lila emphasised. "It also includes how a child fits into the social ecosystem of their world. Our goal is to help children shape their identity consciously rather than inherit it passively."

To close the session, Lila invited parents to form a circle and share what they hoped their child would believe about themselves. Wishes of self-worth, sensitivity, and purpose filled the room. Lila nodded warmly and reminded them that children ultimately come to believe about themselves what they most consistently feel from their caregivers.

As the session ended, parents lingered, speaking more openly and reflectively. Many left with a shift in perspective—not only about their children, but about themselves. The journey of shaping a child's identity, Lila concluded, begins with presence, intention, and love. Every interaction—every boundary, every bedtime story—is part of a sacred unfolding between child, caregiver, and community.

She then spoke about the role of cultural values and parenting styles in identity formation. Culture and parenting, she explained, quietly weave the deepest threads of a child's development. From birth, children absorb expectations, traditions, emotional cues, and social norms that inform who they believe they are. Identity is not merely inherited—it is cultivated and reflected within the home and the broader cultural environment.

Early childhood, she explained, is especially critical because the brain is highly plastic and the subconscious deeply receptive. Between birth and age seven, children absorb experiences as blueprints for understanding life. Emotional responses, habits, moral values, and even spiritual perspectives often take root during these formative years.

Culture offers children their first map of meaning, shaping ideas of right and wrong, strength and vulnerability, belonging and worth. Parenting styles act as translators of these cultural values. Through daily interactions—how rules are enforced, affection is shown, and conflict is handled—children receive powerful messages about themselves and the world.

Lila described the four primary parenting styles—authoritative, authoritarian, permissive, and neglectful—and explained how their effects vary across cultural contexts. What matters most is not the label, but the intersection between culture, intention, and awareness. She went on to speak about habits, reminding parents that identity is shaped not only by values but by repeated behaviours. Children internalise habits of gratitude, fear, reflection, or repression by observing their caregivers. These habits become internal patterns of meaning-making that persist into adulthood.

Society itself, she added, acts as a mirror. Social position, economic class, language, religion, and community status influence how children perceive their place in the world. Conscious caregivers can help children navigate these realities with dignity, humility, and resilience rather than shame or entitlement.

Through examples, Lila illustrated how two children in similar social circumstances can develop vastly different identities depending on their caregivers 'inner work and awareness. Cultural values and parenting styles, she said, are the architects of identity, shaping a child's inner narrative long before they can consciously reflect on it.

Turning to early learning, Lila explained that learning begins long before language. Infants absorb lessons through touch, tone, and emotional attunement. When needs are met with consistency and care, children learn that the world is safe and that they are worthy of love. Caregivers, she emphasised, are the child's first and most influential teachers.

As children grow more conscious, the role of adults remains vital. Emotional attunement, consistency, and presence support healthy cognitive and emotional development. Maturity, she reminded them, is not defined by age but by awareness and regulation.

Play, Lila explained, is the language of childhood. Through play, children explore roles, emotions, problem-solving, and empathy. Play strengthens executive function, emotional regulation, and social understanding. It is not separate from learning—it is learning.

She also spoke about dependence and trust, explaining that secure early relationships allow children to explore the world with confidence. When children feel safe to depend on others, they develop resilience rather than control or anxiety. The emotional environment, she said, becomes a living mirror that reflects what is allowed, valued, and possible.

Finally, Lila spoke of the long arc from early experience to lifelong identity. Early emotional scripts echo into adulthood, shaping relationships, stress responses, and self-worth. Conscious caregiving, she concluded, is a sacred responsibility. Every moment of patience, play, and presence writes an inner message that says: You matter. You are safe. You are free to grow.

As she stepped down from the stage, the room filled with warm applause. Parents smiled, some with misty eyes, sharing a quiet sense of connection and hope. Lila acknowledged them with grace, reminding everyone that every moment with a child is a seed—one that may not bloom immediately, but shapes the future in profound ways.

Chapter 2: Potluck and Parenthood in Community

The Petersons 'house stood at the heart of a thriving, multicultural neighbourhood—a living example of diversity in action. Located on a peaceful cul-de-sac, it was surrounded by families from many parts of the world, their cultures blending seamlessly into daily life. The neighbourhood came alive with a rich mix of sounds, sights, and scents, forming a vibrant picture of shared living. As morning light rose, it cast a golden glow over the area, with the Petersons 'home resting quietly at its centre.

The houses along the street followed a similar suburban design, yet each reflected the heritage of its occupants. The Petersons 'home featured a tidy front-yard garden, while next door lived the Chatterjees, who had immigrated from India two years earlier after Mr. Chatterjee accepted a promising job offer from an American company. Their garden bloomed with jasmine and marigolds, the fragrances drifting gently through the cool morning air. Their home was a graceful expression of their Indian roots.

Mr. Chatterjee, a distinguished man from Bengal, had a deep love for classical music. The melodies of the sitar and the rhythmic beats of the tabla often filled the evenings with warmth and nostalgia. Rabindra Sangeet echoed softly through their home, and frequently the sounds of their children practising music blended with the calm rhythm of the neighbourhood. He was married to Arpita, a graceful Brahmin woman with expressive eyes and a gentle presence. Her commitment to vegetarianism and traditional values reflected her deep cultural grounding. Often dressed in elegant saris, she carried herself with quiet dignity.

The Chatterjees enriched the neighbourhood by sharing the flavours of Bengali cuisine and the depth of Indian classical music with their neighbours. Their story was one of tradition, adaptation, and harmony—an example of how cultures could meet and flourish together.

Each morning, as the Petersons stepped out for their daily walk, neighbours greeted one another warmly. Dew sparkled on the grass as sunlight filtered across the street. The identity of the neighbourhood was shaped not just by diversity, but by the way cultures blended to enhance everyone's lives. The Petersons often found themselves learning something new—whether a tradition, a dish, or a perspective. It was a place of exchange, respect, and friendship.

Ethan and Ben grew up surrounded by this richness. Their environment broadened their worldview, teaching them to appreciate diversity and respect differences through daily exposure to languages, customs, and shared experiences. The neighbourhood was not merely a place to live—it was a community, one that celebrated both individuality and togetherness. It was an ideal place to raise children and instil values of acceptance, respect, and love for all cultures.

Wanting to celebrate the holiday spirit, the Petersons decided to host a potluck for the neighbourhood. Sitting at the kitchen table with lists in hand, Michael and Sarah planned the gathering while Ethan and Ben ran around excitedly. Sarah suggested inviting the Chatterjees to prepare a cultural dish, and Michael agreed enthusiastically. When he called them, Mrs. Chatterjee happily offered to make biryani, much to Sarah's delight.

On the day of the potluck, the Petersons 'home filled with festive aromas and joyful sounds. Ethan and Ben eagerly helped with decorations as the scent of baked cookies, roasting turkey, and pine from the Christmas tree filled the air. Guests arrived carrying dishes from different cultures—biryani, rasgullas, lasagna, and panettone. The table became a colourful feast, reflecting the beauty of shared traditions.

As everyone gathered, laughter and stories flowed freely. Each dish was introduced with its history and meaning, bringing the group closer together. Ethan and Ben listened wide-eyed as they learned about different celebrations and customs. The potluck became more than a meal—it became a celebration of unity, connection, and mutual appreciation.

Later, as the children played together, Michael and Mr. Chatterjee relaxed in the garden. Michael asked how values are instilled when raising children across cultures, particularly noticing differences between siblings. Mr. Chatterjee explained how first-born children often receive intense attention, while younger siblings grow up with more freedom and independence. He noted that siblings naturally support and nurture one another.

Arpita added that each child must be seen as an individual, with unique strengths and needs. Balancing community and individuality allows children to grow while remaining authentic. When Emily, expecting her first child, asked how to ensure an older child still feels valued, Arpita shared the importance of dedicated time and giving each child a voice through simple daily rituals.

William asked about fostering independent self-esteem. Mr. Chatterjee explained that involving children in small decisions builds trust and confidence. Praising effort rather than results helps children see mistakes as part of learning. Sarah reflected that parenting is not about shielding children from challenges, but about teaching them how to navigate them with resilience.

As laughter filled the room—sparked by Ethan and Ben joking about future siblings—the evening slowly settled. Stars shimmered above the Petersons 'home as guests departed. Standing at the doorway, Michael wrapped his arm around Sarah and reflected that the evening had been more than a dinner. It was a reminder that raising children is a shared journey.

Later, as Ethan and Ben drifted to sleep, whispering about food and fun, the Petersons looked around their home, still glowing with togetherness. It had been a day filled with laughter, learning, wisdom, and hope. And in the quiet of the night, they felt a deep sense of comfort, knowing their children were growing up not just in a house, but in a true community.

Chapter 3: Sexuality and Adolescence

The doorbell rang as the Peterson household bustled with holiday preparations. When Sarah opened the door, she found her cousin Emma standing there, her expression tired and tense. Sarah immediately sensed something was wrong. She welcomed Emma inside and guided her to the cozy living room.

"Emma, it's so good to see you," Sarah said gently. "But you look exhausted. What's going on?"

Emma sighed heavily as she settled into a soft armchair. "Sarah," she began, her voice a mix of curiosity and concern, "my daughter asked me something the other day that completely caught me off guard. She asked, 'What is sex? 'I didn't know how to answer her in a way that was honest, scientific, and still appropriate for her age."

Sarah nodded with understanding. "It's a difficult question for many parents," she said. "But it's also an opportunity. You can explain that sex is a form of energy—just like everything else in life. What makes it unique is how it operates through hormones and imagination. This energy shows up differently in everyone and evolves as we grow. It's important for children to understand that sexual energy isn't something to fear or suppress. It's a natural part of being human—an inner fire that draws us toward connection, closeness, and intimacy."

Emma listened closely, nodding. "That actually makes a lot of sense," she said. "But how do different approaches to sexuality education affect children?"

"When children grow up with confusion or silence around sexuality," Sarah explained, "misunderstandings can arise. In societies where these conversations are avoided, imagination often runs unchecked. Without guidance, this can lead to pressure, distorted beliefs, or harmful behaviour. Sexual energy itself isn't the problem—it's the lack of awareness around it."

She continued, "Sexual energy is like fire. When it's understood and respected, it warms and connects. Problems arise when it's acted upon without mutual understanding or consent. Teaching children respect, balance, and awareness—both of themselves and others—helps prevent harm and supports healthier relationships."

Emma reflected quietly. "So it's really about awareness and respect."

"Exactly," Sarah replied. "When we speak openly and honestly, using age-appropriate language, children grow into adults who respect themselves and others."

After a moment, Emma asked, "How can parents encourage healthy awareness of the body, especially at a young age?"

Sarah smiled. "It begins with natural, respectful interaction. Parents who are comfortable with their own bodies model that comfort for their children. Simple acts like gentle massage during early childhood help children become familiar with their bodies in a safe way. As they grow, questions about changes or sensations will arise naturally. When they do, parents should respond calmly and openly."

She added that children should be taught about birth and a woman's natural cycle, including menstruation, long before it begins. "Explain that bleeding is a natural sign of growth. Talk about how pain and pleasure both play roles in development, especially for women. Boys need to hear this too—it helps them develop empathy and understanding for future partners. This shared knowledge encourages respect between genders."

As Michael decorated the Christmas tree, he joined the conversation. "Emma, we're here for you," he said reassuringly. "Tell us what else is on your mind."

Emma smiled, feeling supported. "I keep hearing about hormones," she said. "How do we explain their role in a way children can understand?"

Sarah explained, "Hormones are messengers in the body. They tell different systems what to do—how we grow, when puberty starts, how we feel, and even how we sleep. Understanding hormones helps children make sense of their emotions and physical changes."

Michael added, "Adrenaline helps us respond to danger. Dopamine affects motivation and happiness. Endorphins reduce pain and stress. Insulin regulates blood sugar. Cortisol manages stress, and melatonin controls sleep. When children understand these basics, they feel less overwhelmed by what's happening inside them."

Sarah continued, "Oxytocin supports bonding and connection, while estrogen and testosterone influence physical development and sexual energy. Both hormones exist in everyone—just in different balances."

Emma nodded, impressed. "So how do we help kids manage all these changes?"

"Through emotional intelligence," Sarah replied. "Teach children that these shifts are normal. Help them notice how their feelings connect to their bodies. Encourage open conversations so they don't feel alone or ashamed."

Michael added that children who understand their bodies are more confident and often emerge as leaders among peers. "Knowledge replaces fear with confidence," he said.

Emma then asked about boys experiencing sexual urges. Sarah responded gently, "Boys need safe spaces to talk. Sexual urges are natural. What matters is learning how to manage imagination and energy—by channeling it into creativity, movement, learning, and emotional awareness. Boundaries, consent, and respect must always be part of the conversation."

Michael added that girls should be prepared emotionally and practically for menstruation before it begins. "When girls understand what's coming, fear and shame disappear."

Emma reflected, "Our culture avoids these talks, and that silence creates confusion."

"Yes," Sarah said softly. "Silence creates fear. Openness creates trust."

Finally, Emma asked about same-gender curiosity. Sarah replied calmly, "Curiosity is part of identity exploration. Parents don't need to panic. Ask gentle questions that help children reflect on their feelings. The goal is emotional awareness, not labels."

Michael added, "What children need most is acceptance. When there's no judgment at home, they feel safe to grow into who they truly are."

The room grew quiet as they sipped their tea, connected by a shared purpose. As the Christmas lights twinkled softly, Emma smiled and said, "Thank you. This conversation has changed how I see everything."

Sarah smiled back. "You're not alone. And neither are your children."

Chapter 4: Community and Belonging

The Chatterjees and the Petersons were next-door neighbours who, over the years, had built a deep and meaningful friendship. Though they came from different cultural and religious backgrounds—the Petersons being Christians and the Chatterjees practising Hinduism—their bond grew through shared values, mutual respect, and genuine care for one another. They often gathered for dinners, celebrated each other's festivals, and stood by one another through life's joys and challenges.

They had first met at a community function, where conversation gradually revealed how much they had in common despite their differences. Values such as compassion, respect, and the importance of family formed a strong foundation for their friendship. Their families spent time together at local parks, attended each other's celebrations, and created space for curiosity and learning. This cross-cultural relationship offered both families a rich opportunity to understand and appreciate different traditions and beliefs.

One Sunday morning, as Ethan and Ben played in the front yard, Mrs. Chatterjee greeted Sarah Peterson with a warm smile. As they chatted, Arpita invited the Petersons to Anika's birthday celebration planned for that evening. The gathering was arranged in the backyard, where cool breezes and birdsong created a peaceful atmosphere.

As the children played, Arpita noticed a troubled expression on Ethan's face. Gently, she asked what was bothering him. Ethan hesitated before admitting that he had an upcoming essay competition at school on the topic of religion and beliefs, and he felt completely unsure of how to begin.

Arpita listened with empathy. She reassured him that while the topic might feel overwhelming, it was also an opportunity to reflect and learn. She encouraged Ethan to start with what he knew—his own beliefs and traditions—and then explore how different families, like theirs, practiced faith in unique ways. She suggested writing about how understanding and respecting differences had strengthened the friendship between their families.

Sarah nodded in agreement, adding that every individual has the right to their own beliefs and that faith is a personal choice deserving respect. Michael shared that they had always taught their children that faith is a personal journey and that respecting others 'choices creates a sense of safety and harmony in the community.

Arpita added that within their family, everyone was encouraged to ask questions, express ideas, and even participate in one another's customs. This openness, she explained, helped build security, understanding, and respect.

Ethan's face brightened as confidence replaced uncertainty. He realised he could write about celebrating Diwali with the Chatterjees and Christmas with his own family—how learning from one another had deepened their bond. Grateful for Arpita's guidance, he felt ready to share his thoughts on diversity and mutual respect.

Later, Sarah expressed her appreciation to Arpita and suggested they continue discussing ways to meaningfully share customs and beliefs with their children. Over tea, the conversation turned reflective.

The next day, Sarah asked Arpita a thoughtful question: how could parents raise children with strong moral and ethical values while still grounding them in a religious tradition? Arpita responded that religion can offer a framework for morality, stability, and belonging that extends beyond national boundaries. In an increasingly interconnected world, this sense of global belonging can be deeply valuable.

However, she emphasised that religion should not be presented as the sole source of morality. Ethics, she explained, must be universal and inclusive. Parents can help children understand why religions exist—how they arose to meet human needs for meaning, guidance, and community. When children learn to view religion as one perspective among many, they develop respect for diversity and avoid rigid thinking.

Arpita cautioned that an overly exclusive attachment to one belief system can be harmful. Encouraging children to explore different religions and philosophies fosters critical thinking and global citizenship, while still allowing them to honour their own heritage.

Sarah reflected on how confusing religion can be for children, especially when they encounter many belief systems and strict traditions. Arpita acknowledged this challenge and stressed the importance of creating an atmosphere of respect and open dialogue. At its best, she said, religion serves as a tool for self-reflection and community building. When paired with universal ethics, it enriches life without limiting understanding.

Sarah added that understanding does not require changing one's beliefs—it simply means respecting others'. Acceptance, she said, is about creating space for everyone to exist without fear of judgment or exclusion.

Arpita smiled warmly, agreeing that when children feel secure in their identity and open to learning about others, parents lay the foundation for a more inclusive and compassionate world.

Michael, who had been listening quietly, shared that he appreciated how curiosity naturally arose when the children interacted. What mattered most, he observed, was that they learned to ask questions with respect rather than judgment.

"That's the key," Arpita agreed. Encouraging respectful questions, she explained, helps prevent prejudice and misunderstanding before they take root. When parents model openness and curiosity, children follow naturally.

As the sun set, casting a soft golden glow across the backyard, the families continued sharing tea and laughter while the children played nearby. In that quiet moment, their bond stood as a living example of true community and belonging—one that transcended religion and culture, grounded instead in empathy, respect, and shared human values.

Chapter 5: Safety and Security

The ABC Club, known for its commitment to community engagement and child development, organized a workshop for parents on the theme "Ensuring Safety and Security for Children." The club regularly hosts sessions on parenting, education, and overall well-being, and this particular event drew enthusiastic participation from parents eager to learn how to better protect and support their children.

The session began with a warm welcome and the introduction of the guests of honor. The keynote speaker, well known for her expertise in child safety and emotional well-being, was felicitated amidst applause. The audience settled in with anticipation as the session began.

The speaker emphasized that child safety and security are among the most critical responsibilities in today's complex world. She explained that while parents and communities cannot eliminate all risks, they can equip children with awareness, confidence, and emotional strength. The session, she noted, was intended to help parents understand potential dangers, foster open communication, and empower children to navigate challenges in a safe and supportive environment.

Emma raised concerns about child trafficking and kidnapping, pointing out that modern life often makes it impossible for parents to be physically present with their children at all times. The counsclor acknowledged this reality and explained that safety is not about constant supervision alone. Parents must establish clear boundaries and teach children how to stay safe both at home and outside. While physical precautions such as secure doors and supervision are important, she stressed that true safety begins with personal integrity. When children understand their own boundaries and feel confident asserting them, they are better protected.

William then asked about the psychological and emotional aspects of child safety. Dr. Priya Mehta explained that trust plays a central role. Children must learn not just to trust, but to understand whom to trust and why. She highlighted the confusion children often experience when parents warn them against strangers while also encouraging social interaction. A balanced approach, she explained, is essential, with parents modeling safe behavior and guiding children during interactions with unfamiliar people.

Dr. Mehta also spoke about loneliness as a significant vulnerability. Children who feel isolated can become easy targets, especially in the digital age where interaction often happens online and alone. Teaching children to seek companionship in safe environments and avoid risky isolation is an essential part of emotional safety.

The importance of boundaries was emphasized again as Dr. Mehta explained that curiosity is natural but should be explored within safe, trusted spaces. Awareness and guidance help children navigate the world without fear.

Mark asked how parents could set limits that were neither too strict nor too permissive. Dr. Mehta explained that boundaries should guide rather than confine. Every child is different, and parents must observe their readiness to handle responsibility. She gave an example of a child learning through experience, such as touching something hot under supervision. Such moments allow children to learn safely without excessive restriction.

She stressed that children learn more from what parents do than from what they say. When parents act with caution, balance, and consistency, children naturally absorb those qualities. Limits should be flexible and evolve as children grow. Overly rigid rules can suppress creativity, while excessive freedom can leave children unprepared. Explaining rules fosters trust and mutual respect.

Sarah raised concerns about inconsistent or indulgent parenting. Dr. Mehta agreed that unpredictability can confuse children and lead them to take risks without understanding consequences. Clear, consistent boundaries help children assess danger and make informed decisions. Parenting, she reminded the group, is not about perfection but about mindful consistency.

Michael then asked about teaching self-defense. Dr. Mehta introduced Mr. James Carter, a self-defense instructor, who explained that self-defense begins with awareness and parental involvement. Children learn best through observation, so parents should model safety behaviors. Teaching situational awareness, avoiding unsafe isolation, setting boundaries, and trusting instincts are all essential elements of self-defense.

Mr. Carter emphasized that self-defense is not about aggression but about calm decision-making and knowing when to walk away. Role-playing scenarios help children practice safe responses and build confidence.

After a short break, parents discussed the session in small groups, sharing reflections on how practical advice could transform daily parenting. Mr. Carter then explained how to recognize signs of danger, such as alarms, unusual sounds, or changes in behavior. He stressed the importance of preparation through simple drills, such as evacuation plans and regroup points, which build instinctive responses in emergencies.

The session continued with discussions on emotional safety, particularly anger and frustration in teenagers. Dr. Mehta explained that anger often stems from deeper issues such as pressure, unmet expectations, or feeling unheard. Parents can help by encouraging children to identify and name their emotions, channel anger constructively, and use healthy outlets such as physical activity or reflection.

She emphasized that emotions themselves are not harmful, but unmanaged reactions can be. Teaching children to pause, reflect, and communicate helps reduce emotional outbursts. Parental modeling, storytelling, and role-playing were recommended as effective tools for emotional regulation.

When asked about impulse control, Dr. Mehta shared simple techniques such as controlled breathing and counting before reacting. These practices create space between impulse and action, helping children regulate emotions more effectively.

Later in the session, Dr. Jane Thompson spoke about providing stability during stressful times. She explained that routine and predictability give children a sense of safety, especially during transitions. Secure environments help children develop resilience, confidence, and healthy relationships.

The discussion concluded with reflections on creating peaceful homes through mindfulness and presence. Mr. Prakash introduced mindfulness as the practice of being fully aware in the present moment. He explained that cultivating calm thoughts and positive intentions builds inner strength, which naturally extends to family life.

The workshop ended on a reflective note, with parents leaving equipped with practical tools and renewed awareness. The session reinforced that safety is not rooted in fear but in preparation, presence, emotional connection, and love. When children feel secure, heard, and supported, they are better prepared to face the world with confidence and resilience.

Chapter 6: Family Dynamics and Influence

Some months later, the ABC Club launched its next eagerly anticipated session. Having developed a deep connection during earlier discussions, parents returned with genuine interest and openness. This time, the topic touched a place close to every heart—family dynamics and their impact. Curiosity filled the room as parents prepared to explore how everyday interactions within the home shape a child's emotional world, identity, and lifelong relationship patterns.

The familiar community hall buzzed softly with conversation as families gathered once again. Following the success of previous workshops, there was a shared eagerness to engage with a theme that reflected the very essence of family life.

As the murmurs settled, Counsellor Ava Mitchell, a seasoned child and family therapist known for her compassionate and intuitive guidance, stepped forward with a warm smile.

"Welcome back, everyone," Ava began gently. "Today's question is simple, yet profound: Do parenting styles affect a child's moral, social, and emotional development?"

She paused before continuing. "The answer is yes—but not in a surface-level or one-size-fits-all way. The deeper truth is this: a child becomes a reflection of the guardian's inner world. What we do, who we are, how we feel, and how we navigate life—these are what children absorb, both consciously and unconsciously. Not what we tell them, but what we show them."

Ava explained that from the very beginning, children learn primarily through observation. More than words or instruction, they absorb emotional patterns, behavioural responses, and even the unspoken energy of their caregivers. A parent may speak of compassion, but if impatience or judgment is consistently modelled, that is the energy a child internalises.

"Children don't do what we say," Ava said. "They do what we are. Every habit, emotional reaction, unresolved wound, or silent tension ripple into a child's experience."

She emphasized that this is why a parent's self-awareness and emotional maturity are so vital. The more conscious and integrated the caregiver, the more stable and loving the environment becomes—not just externally, but at a deeper level. Children, she reminded the group, are not blank slates. They arrive with their own essence, lessons, and timing.

Many emotional habits are passed down unconsciously. A parent raised to suppress emotions may unknowingly teach the same. A guardian who fears failure may instil pressure or control. Yet the opposite is also true. A parent who embodies calm, presence, and compassion equips their child with a grounded and morally sound inner world.

"That's why parenting is less about teaching," Ava explained, "and more about vibration. It's about who we are being, not just what we are doing."

She invited parents to view parenting as a shared journey rather than a role of authority. Families, she suggested, are formed not only by biology but by deeper purpose. Some come together to heal, some to resolve long-standing patterns, and others simply to learn love anew. Not all growth unfolds within one lifetime, but every interaction contributes to something larger.

In today's fast-paced, achievement-driven world, Ava observed that many decisions are rooted in fear—fear of falling behind, of not being enough, of losing control. When parenting is driven by fear, it often results in comparison, pressure, and anxiety. Children raised in such environments may learn to please others, hide their authentic selves, or push beyond their natural rhythm.

Parenting from love, on the other hand, means trusting a child's individual timing. It means offering structure without rigidity, guidance without control, and discipline balanced with compassion. It means allowing children to stumble and being present—not to remove pain, but to help them understand it. Most importantly, it requires healing fear within oneself.

"If you want your child to be emotionally intelligent," Ava said, "be emotionally present. If you want them to be moral, live with integrity. If you want them to be socially confident, show them what authentic connection looks like—starting with yourself."

She reminded parents that children look to their first caregivers for answers to fundamental questions: Is the world safe? Can I trust others? Am I allowed to be myself? A guardian who listens and responds with care teaches a child to embrace life rather than fear it.

"Parenting is not just about raising a child," Ava concluded. "It's about elevating your own inner state so your presence becomes a sanctuary."

After a short break, the session resumed with renewed attentiveness. Sarah, a mother of two, asked how sibling relationships influence identity development and conflict resolution, especially when children are very different from one another.

Ava explained that sibling relationships are deeply formative and rarely accidental. Siblings are often part of a shared journey designed for growth, challenge, and reflection. From early competition for attention to shared secrets and rivalry, siblings provide a child's first experience of belonging and contrast.

"All bonds are purposeful," Ava said. "You don't get siblings by accident. You get the ones necessary for your growth."

She explained that siblings act as mirrors, sometimes offering support and sometimes friction. Even when raised in the same household, each child interprets experiences through a unique inner lens. Understanding this individuality helps move families away from comparison and toward empathy.

Parents, she noted, play a crucial role by honouring each child's uniqueness and modelling emotional maturity. When differences are seen as strengths rather than competition, siblings learn to complement rather than compete.

The conversation later turned to culture and values when Mrs. Chatterjee asked how customs influence attitudes and behaviour. Counsellor Rayan Silva responded, explaining that culture forms an invisible framework for identity, offering both grounding and direction.

For families rooted in their ancestral land, culture is woven into daily life. For those living away from their origins, traditions often become anchors—symbols of belonging and continuity. However, Rayan emphasized that culture must be engaged with consciously. Unquestioned traditions can limit growth, while rejected traditions can leave children unanchored.

"Maturity," he explained, "allows us to carry culture with awareness—honouring what nourishes us and letting go of what no longer serves."

He likened children to trees whose roots are values and customs. When roots are nourished—whether through lived tradition or meaningful memory—children develop resilience and clarity. Culture, he said, should be a companion, not a cage.

Later, Mr. Chatterjee asked about family communication and emotional security. Rayan responded that communication is the foundation of trust and belonging. True communication is not about logistics, but about presence. When children feel genuinely heard, they feel valued.

He introduced the idea of intentional listening—creating space for expression without interruption or judgment. Silence, he explained, is sometimes mistaken for strength but often reflects fear or emotional withdrawal. Healing begins when families create safe spaces where emotions can be expressed openly.

The session closed with a difficult but important question about dysfunctional families and long-term mental health. Rayan acknowledged that unstable environments can leave deep emotional imprints, though each child's experience is shaped by their inner resilience and awareness.

In families where caregivers are emotionally grounded, children learn trust and self-worth. In more fragmented environments, children may take on roles beyond their readiness. Yet even in dysfunction, Rayan reminded the group, growth is possible. No experience is wasted, and healing can begin at any point through awareness and presence.

As the evening came to a close, the room remained quiet and reflective. Parents left not with answers alone, but with a deeper understanding that family life is not about perfection—it is about consciousness.

In nurturing their children, they were also invited to nurture themselves.

Chapter 7: Emotional Awareness and Inner Growth

As the journey of reflection continued, the ABC Club introduced another session that invited parents to turn their attention inward. This chapter explored emotional awareness—not just as a skill to be taught to children, but as a way of being that begins within the adult. The atmosphere was calm and contemplative, setting the tone for a deeper exploration of inner growth and emotional responsibility.

The facilitator began by explaining that emotions are not obstacles to be managed or suppressed, but messages that guide understanding. Children, she noted, are naturally emotionally expressive. They cry, laugh, resist, and question freely. Over time, however, many children learn to silence their emotions—not because they lack feelings, but because they sense discomfort or rejection around emotional expression.

"When emotions are dismissed," she explained, "children don't stop feeling. They stop sharing."

Emotional awareness begins when parents recognize and accept their own inner experiences. A child who grows up witnessing adults acknowledging emotions—without blame, fear, or judgment—learns that feelings are safe and temporary. Such children develop resilience not by avoiding emotions, but by learning how to move through them.

Parents often asked how to respond to intense emotions like anger, sadness, or fear. The facilitator emphasized that emotions do not require fixing. They require presence. When a child feels seen and heard, emotional intensity naturally softens. Trying to reason, correct, or distract too quickly can unintentionally communicate that emotions are unacceptable.

She encouraged parents to name emotions gently. Simple reflections such as "I see that you are upset" or "This feels hard for you right now" help children develop emotional vocabulary and self-understanding. Over time, children learn to identify their feelings instead of being overwhelmed by them.

The discussion then turned to emotional regulation. Regulation, the facilitator clarified, is not control. It is the ability to stay connected to oneself during emotional experiences. Children learn regulation through co-regulation—being soothed by a calm, grounded adult. A dysregulated adult cannot guide a child toward calm.

"Your nervous system becomes their reference point," she said.

Parents were invited to reflect on how stress, exhaustion, and unresolved emotions influence their responses. Many moments of conflict, she explained, are less about the child's behaviour and more about the adult's capacity in that moment. Awareness of this shifts parenting from reaction to response.

The session also addressed emotional conditioning. Children quickly learn which emotions are acceptable and which are not, often based on subtle cues. Praise, withdrawal, comparison, or silence all teach emotional lessons. When certain emotions are consistently discouraged, children may disconnect from parts of themselves to maintain attachment.

Inner growth, therefore, is not only a child's task—it is an adult's responsibility. When parents allow themselves to feel fully and heal consciously, they break cycles of emotional suppression passed through generations.

One parent asked how to support children through emotional pain without becoming overwhelmed themselves. The facilitator explained that compassion does not mean absorbing a child's emotions. It means holding space while staying rooted in one's own centre. Boundaries, she reminded, protect both the child and the adult.

The chapter also explored how emotional awareness supports empathy and healthy relationships. Children who understand their own emotions are better able to recognize emotions in others. This awareness fosters kindness, accountability, and emotional intelligence—skills far more valuable than perfection or performance.

As the conversation deepened, the facilitator emphasized patience. Emotional growth unfolds gradually. There is no shortcut and no ideal timeline. What matters most is consistency, honesty, and presence.

The session closed with a reminder that emotional awareness is not about creating emotionally "perfect" children. It is about raising humans who feel safe within themselves.

When children are allowed to experience their emotions without fear, they grow into adults who can meet life with clarity, compassion, and inner strength.

Chapter 8: Foundations of a Good Life

On a cold Saturday morning, the Chatterjees and the Petersons decided to volunteer at a nearby food bank. The air was crisp, and the warmth of families coming together to support their community filled the space. It was the first time both families had brought their children along, making the experience especially meaningful.

As they arrived, the children—Raj, Anika, Ben, and Ethan—looked around with curiosity and excitement. They observed the stacks of food, the busy volunteers, and the steady stream of people arriving for support. Gathering the children close, Mr. Chatterjee and Michael explained why they were there. They spoke about responsibility, community, and the importance of ensuring that everyone has access to basic necessities. Through simple words and calm presence, they introduced the idea of social responsibility—not as an obligation, but as an act of care.

The children were assigned small tasks based on their abilities. Some sorted canned goods, others packed boxes. As they worked, Sarah and Arpita gently explained how these efforts mattered. They spoke about how each box of food would help families through difficult times and how community thrives when people support one another. The children began to feel proud, noticing gratitude in the eyes of those they were helping.

After hours of work, the families paused to rest and reflect. Elizabeth Turner, a member of the organizing committee, observed the children with admiration and asked the parents what values they believed were essential for leading a good life. Arpita responded thoughtfully, naming honesty, self-knowledge, and self-respect as foundational virtues. She reflected on how parents create a life manual for their children—not through instructions, but through attentive presence, observation, and understanding.

She explained that a balanced life grows from knowing oneself and acting with integrity. When individuals respect themselves and live honestly, relationships deepen naturally over time. Trust builds gradually, much like peeling layers of an onion, revealing understanding and connection beneath. These values, she added, help children learn how to balance their own needs with those of others, shaping them into contributors to society.

When asked how children develop these values, Arpita emphasized that parents can only teach what they embody. Children observe far more than adults realize. Honesty, self-awareness, and self-respect, when lived by parents, become natural lessons for children. She shared that when parents openly express thoughts and emotions, children learn to do the same without fear. Personal growth practices—such as mindfulness, learning, or creative exploration—benefit children indirectly by modeling maturity and self-development.

She also acknowledged that some children face emotional or behavioral challenges. In such cases, patience, understanding, and professional support become essential. Building values, she said, is a long-term process that requires consistency, love, and open communication.

The children, moved by the experience, shared their thoughts. They spoke about how good it felt to help and expressed a desire to do more. Their parents smiled, recognizing that these moments would stay with them for a lifetime, shaping how they viewed kindness and responsibility.

The conversation then turned to morality. Sarah explained that moral character is not about rigid rules but about living with awareness of right and wrong. Children learn honesty, kindness, and respect by observing how adults treat others and handle responsibility. Ownership, accountability, and respect for both people and possessions are learned through daily experiences at home.

As discussions continued, the parents explored empathy, compassion, and justice. These values, they agreed, cannot be rushed or forced. They are best learned through real-life experiences—sharing, waiting, negotiating, and understanding emotions as they arise. Such moments, though small, form the foundation of empathy and fairness.

Emotional intelligence emerged as another key theme. Mr. Chatterjee explained that self-awareness and self-respect allow children to navigate challenges with confidence and empathy. Creative methods such as art and mindful expression help children explore emotions safely and authentically, teaching acceptance, balance, and letting go.

The parents reflected on how emotional intelligence is not only a child's journey but an adult's as well. When parents admit their own gaps and continue learning, children see growth as strength rather than weakness.

Later, concerns arose about external influences—friends, digital spaces, and societal pressures. The parents discussed the importance of modeling healthy relationships, maintaining open communication, and staying involved without control. By listening without judgment, parents can guide children toward supportive and respectful connections.

The discussion expanded to work habits, responsibility, and financial awareness. Children, it was noted, thrive when they feel valued and trusted. Teaching balance between the digital and real world helps them develop rhythm and discipline. Financial literacy, introduced early through everyday examples and simple games, equips children with confidence and independence.

The chapter also addressed respect for laws and boundaries. Parents agreed that children should learn age-appropriate understanding of rules, justice, and consequences—first at home, then in society. Clear boundaries, consistency, and accountability create a moral structure that supports emotional and social well-being.

As the day came to an end, the families returned to their tasks while the children played, laughed, and formed new friendships. The experience had quietly planted seeds of awareness, compassion, and responsibility.

The foundation of a good life, they realized, is not built through lectures or perfection. It is built through lived values, shared experiences, and conscious presence. When adults choose to live with honesty, respect, and awareness, children naturally reflect those qualities—carrying them forward into the world.

Chapter 9: Becoming an Adult

The Peterson family sat quietly around their kitchen table, concern evident on every face. Ben sat with his head down, nervously picking at the edge of his notebook. Sarah watched him closely before gently asking what had been troubling him at school. At first, Ben brushed it off, but when Michael reassured him that he was not alone, his voice cracked. He admitted that other children teased him about his body and that he no longer wanted to go to school. Shame and sadness filled the room as Ben struggled to meet their eyes.

Ethan tried to encourage his brother, reminding him that others' opinions did not define him. But Ben felt misunderstood. To him, the pain was real and heavy. Michael placed a reassuring hand on Ben's shoulder and promised that they would face the situation together, including speaking with his teachers and finding supportive solutions.

Later that evening, Sarah and Michael sat in the garden, reflecting on Ben's struggles. They acknowledged how deeply body image and self-esteem affect children, especially during puberty—a time when physical and emotional changes can feel overwhelming. Michael emphasized the importance of helping Ben understand that his worth was not tied to appearance. With patience, reassurance, and understanding, they believed he could learn to accept himself and develop confidence in social interactions.

That night, they spoke with Ben in his room, where he was quietly drawing. Sarah sat beside him and gently explained that feeling timid or afraid was natural and did not make him weak or different. She spoke about the body as a remarkable system that constantly communicates its needs and reminded him that caring for it was an act of respect, not judgment.

Michael added that bodies change throughout life and that what Ben was experiencing was part of a larger journey. Everyone's body, he reminded him, is unique, and that uniqueness is something to be valued. Sarah suggested practices such as quiet reflection, prayer, or meditation as ways to connect with one's body and emotions without needing external validation.

They explained that adolescence brings hormonal changes that often lead to self-comparison, confusion, and insecurity. Relationships also become more complex as teenagers explore boundaries with peers and family while trying to understand who they are. What mattered most, they assured Ben, was open communication and the freedom to express feelings without fear of judgment.

When Ben hesitantly asked if it was acceptable to be overweight, Michael reassured him that taking care of both body and mind was what truly mattered. Healthy habits, rest, and kindness toward oneself were more important than comparison. Everyone, he reminded Ben, faces challenges, and growth comes from how those challenges are handled.

Sarah encouraged Ben to focus on the present rather than worrying excessively about the future or others 'opinions. She spoke of her own difficult experiences and how they had shaped her strength. Life's challenges, she said, often become stepping stones for growth. Although Ben still felt uncertain, he agreed to try. His parents then discussed whether traditional schooling was supporting his emotional needs. They considered alternative learning environments while agreeing that any decision should involve Ben and prioritize emotional well-being rather than avoidance.

The following evening, the Chatterjees visited. Mr. Chatterjee gently suggested that changing schools alone would not solve the issue. What Ben needed most was a deep sense of connection and understanding. He encouraged Sarah and Michael to listen closely to Ben's thoughts, avoid imposing expectations, and help him explore his interests practically and honestly.

Mrs. Chatterjee added that building inner strength mattered more than removing challenges entirely. Children grow when they feel supported, not shielded. Exploring interests together—through museums, documentaries, reading, and hands-on activities—teaches curiosity, resilience, and confidence.

Over time, Ben began expressing himself through drawing and writing. His teacher, Mrs. Williams, noticed his talent and encouraged him to share his work with the class. Though nervous at first, Ben gained confidence as his classmates listened and responded positively. For the first time, he felt a sense of belonging.

At home, open conversations continued. Michael shared stories from his own childhood, emphasizing that progress comes through guidance and patience, not perfection. He reminded Ben that mentors—teachers, coaches, or guides—can make a profound difference, and that discovering one's strengths takes time.

Ben slowly began to feel more secure. Though nervous moments remained, he learned to express his feelings and trust his growth. When faced with peer pressure to skip school, Ben turned to his parents for guidance. Together, they discussed values, long-term consequences, and the strength required to say no when something felt wrong.

Michael and Sarah reinforced that mistakes are part of learning and that flexibility in life choices is essential. What mattered most was staying true to one's values and learning from experience rather than seeking approval.

As Ben prepared for school the next day, he felt more confident in his decisions. His parents watched with quiet pride, knowing that these conversations were shaping resilience and integrity.

One evening, Ben showed them a drawing of himself standing at the center of a vibrant landscape. He explained that it represented his growing ability to express himself. Sarah and Michael realized how emotional support, patience, and understanding had strengthened not only Ben's confidence but also their family bond.

During a weekend gathering, the Petersons and Chatterjees reflected on the growing pressures children face in a rapidly changing world. They discussed social media, comparison, success, and the importance of grounding children in self-awareness rather than external validation. Both families agreed that balance—between ambition and well-being, independence and guidance—was essential.

They spoke about teaching children financial awareness, responsibility, and critical thinking, as well as the importance of rest, joy, and mental health. Success, they agreed, is not defined by comparison but by alignment with personal values.

As the evening unfolded, the families shared stories, laughter, and quiet reflection. They recognized that parenting is a continuous journey of presence, patience, and learning. By offering their children safe spaces, honest communication, and the freedom to grow at their own pace, they were helping them step into adulthood with confidence and compassion.

As the sun set over the garden, the parents felt reassured. Though the path to adulthood is rarely straight, they knew that with empathy, openness, and trust, their children were developing the strength to navigate life with courage, resilience, and self-belief.

Chapter 10: Life Transitions

It was a warm evening, filled with the scent of freshly cooked biryani and gentle laughter, as the Chatterjees and Petersons sat around the dinner table. After a week-long separation, their discussions naturally turned to personal updates and upcoming travel plans.

During dessert, Mr. Peterson leaned forward with interest and asked about the sudden trip to India planned for the following month. Mr. Chatterjee sighed softly and explained that their parents needed support. His mother's health had been fragile for some time, and managing daily life had become increasingly difficult for them. Being present felt necessary.

Mrs. Peterson nodded with understanding and reflected on how such moments often make people think deeply about life. She then asked what kinds of life changes people most commonly experience.

Mr. Chatterjee explained that life transitions are not limited to major events like immigration or retirement. They also include subtle yet profound shifts—changes in appearance, fashion, housing, schooling, interests, and social circles. People enter and exit our lives continuously, and at a deeper level, birth and death themselves represent transitions of the soul. Whether embodied or not, human existence is always moving through phases of transformation.

He shared that how individuals respond to these changes depends largely on emotional maturity and wisdom. Those who are grounded in self-awareness and understand life's rhythms tend to navigate transitions with greater ease. Still, every transition stirs emotions. Even when change is positive, there is grief in letting go of the familiar—habits, relationships, and former versions of oneself.

Awareness during these periods is essential.

Rushing through transitions, he noted, often creates inner chaos. Life has a natural pace, yet many people try to escape discomfort too quickly. Transitions are sacred pauses—times when new information is forming and important choices must be made. Slowing down allows clarity to emerge.

When change is self-initiated, such as a career shift or relocation, people usually give themselves time to adjust. However, unexpected changes imposed by circumstances can feel destabilizing. In such moments, holding firmly to one's inner identity and chosen role becomes vital. Likewise, when a person evolves into a new role or version of themselves, it is important to allow the surrounding environment time to adapt. Life, he concluded, is an ongoing experiment, and every shift invites deeper self-discovery.

The conversation turned toward the importance of social support during transitions. Mrs. Chatterjee explained that supportive networks are essential, especially during major life changes. She described the value of "mirror partners"—people who reflect one's inner and outer experiences with honesty, empathy, and clarity.

She added that humans naturally seek belonging and context. Alongside physical relationships, she also acknowledged the presence of intangible or spiritual supports that offer guidance from a higher perspective during uncertain times. Though unseen, these supports can be deeply stabilizing.

Physical touch, she noted, also plays a significant role in calming the nervous system—whether through a gentle presence or healing touch. Equally important is honesty. If individuals do not express what they are experiencing, others cannot offer meaningful support.

Clear communication about one's internal and external state allows the right kind of help to emerge.

Ultimately, she emphasized that self-awareness is key. Understanding one's own needs enables others to support effectively. When individuals are centered within themselves and surrounded by supportive mirrors—physical or energetic—transformation becomes less frightening.

Mrs. Peterson then asked about the mental processes involved in transitions such as adolescence or career changes. Mrs. Chatterjee explained that transitions are deeply reflective periods centered on identity and role formation. Questions like "Who am I?" become louder, and self-perception is either reinforced or reshaped.

Adolescence, she explained, involves intense internal and external changes, including hormonal shifts, brain development, and emerging identity. These changes often create emotional turbulence and vulnerability. Mature caregivers who share their own experiences can serve as gentle mirrors, helping adolescents feel less isolated.

When external support is lacking, individuals often turn inward or toward spiritual guidance. Genuine intention and openness can invite the right people—mentors, friends, or even strangers—into one's life at the right moment. Career transitions follow a similar pattern, involving not just a change of work but a redefinition of purpose, values, and contribution to the world.

She encouraged welcoming transitions with humility rather than resistance, viewing them not as punishments but as invitations to grow. Such journeys not only deepen self-understanding but also inspire others through lived example.

The discussion then shifted to uncertainty and growth. Mrs. Chatterjee explained that discomfort often arises from fear—of the unknown, of losing control, or of disappointing others. When external voices overpower the inner compass, uncertainty grows. Slowing down, reflecting inwardly, and reconnecting with one's values help restore clarity.

Prayer or intention-setting, she explained, is not wishful thinking but a way of aligning with deeper purpose. It opens space for insight, helping individuals release what no longer serves them and move toward growth.

Mr. Chatterjee added that discernment in relationships is crucial. People act as mirrors—some reflect truth, others distort it. Choosing neutral, compassionate mirrors helps maintain clarity. Life itself, he said, is like a house of mirrors. Learning to laugh at distortions transforms fear into wisdom.

Mrs. Chatterjee concluded that change and uncertainty are not enemies but sacred pauses calling for realignment. When embraced consciously, they strengthen rather than shake foundations, fostering resilience, flexibility, humility, and trust.

When asked about strategies for handling identity shifts, she advised gradual, mindful adjustment—slowing down rather than rushing through change. Establishing grounding routines provides stability amid upheaval. Honest self-assessment across emotional, mental, physical, and spiritual dimensions supports wise decision-making.

She emphasized sharing truth with discernment, protecting the process from unnecessary exposure, and staying focused on one's own journey without becoming entangled in others'. Everyone evolves at their own pace.

She ended with a gentle reminder to enjoy the journey. Identity shifts are natural parts of being human—opportunities to learn, reinvent, and grow. With grace and joy, one can continue forward, aligned with an ever-evolving sense of self.

Chapter 11: Rewriting the Inner Narrative

Mr. Peterson encountered Mr. Chatterjee on a peaceful afternoon, about a week after the Chatterjees returned from India. They sat together on the porch, the gentle spring air moving quietly around them. Mr. Peterson placed a comforting hand on Mr. Chatterjee's shoulder and spoke softly, acknowledging the effort it took to remain strong and expressing sorrow for the loss of his mother. He recognized the weight of grief that accompanies such a farewell.

Mr. Chatterjee nodded slowly, his eyes fixed on the garden ahead. He admitted that witnessing his mother's passing had altered something deep within him. Though he appeared composed, the pain lingered beneath the surface, masked by routine and courtesy. Mr. Peterson sensed this quiet burden and, a few days later, gently suggested attending a reflective session together—not therapy, but a space for discussing life, purpose, and peace. After some hesitation, Mr. Chatterjee agreed.

During the session, the theme of patience emerged. Participants were invited to reflect on the internal and external factors that shape patience. Mr. Johnson explained that patience is not merely a trait, but a process rooted in inner clarity and outer wisdom. The clearer one understands who they are and who they aspire to become, the more resilient they are against chaos and emotional turbulence. Self-knowledge, he said, becomes an anchor during grief, stress, and confusion.

He expanded on the idea that people wear various "uniforms"—not only physical clothing, but emotional and social personas. What individuals choose to reveal reflects their boundaries and intentions.

Even colors and symbols influence how one is received by others. Awareness of how one wishes to engage with the world strengthens the ability to pause, observe, and respond thoughtfully rather than react impulsively.

Mr. Johnson then described the outer world as a complex system, comparing it to a commercial airplane where pilots, engineers, crew, and air traffic control all play essential roles. Patience arises from understanding that no single person controls everything. Recognizing one's role, respecting others 'timing, and trusting the process cultivates calm and balance.

This analogy resonated deeply with Mr. Chatterjee. Though his grief was still fresh, understanding that healing itself was a system—where sorrow, memory, love, and time each had a role—helped him breathe more freely. Patience, he realized, was not passive waiting but honoring each stage with trust in life's unfolding.

As the room settled into quiet reflection, Mr. Peterson encouraged Mr. Chatterjee to voice the question weighing on his heart. After a moment of silence, Mr. Chatterjee asked how people cope positively with trauma, loss, or failure.

Mr. Johnson acknowledged the depth of the question and explained that much suffering arises not from events themselves, but from unmet expectations. Trauma becomes embedded when the mind repeatedly replays what "should have been." Healing begins when one reframes the experience from a broader, more compassionate perspective. Each individual, he emphasized, holds the authority to rewrite their internal narrative in ways that support growth rather than pain.

Speaking about loss, he explained that it often stems from the illusion of permanence. Life is transient, and the healthiest response is to live fully in the present—appreciating what exists while it is there. Mourning is necessary, but gratitude for shared time allows one to move forward without denying love or memory.

When addressing failure, he reframed it as incomplete information or unrealistic expectations. Failure, he said, becomes a teacher when approached with honesty and curiosity. Reflecting on what went wrong, adjusting methods, and learning from experience builds an internal reference system that strengthens wisdom and resilience over time.

He also highlighted the importance of honoring endings. Closure, he explained, is not only emotional but spiritual. Reflecting on what has ended, acknowledging lessons learned, and offering gratitude creates space for new beginnings.

The room grew quiet again as these insights settled. Mr. Chatterjee felt the weight he carried soften slightly—not gone, but lighter—as if he had been given permission to begin healing.

As the session continued, the conversation deepened. Mr. Peterson reflected on how mindset and belief systems often shape outcomes more than external conditions. He asked how beliefs influence resilience and the ability to overcome obstacles.

Mr. Johnson explained that mindsets form the foundation of all change. Thoughts are not random; they are the scripts through which life is lived. When internal narratives are rooted in limitation, behavior follows accordingly. But when beliefs are grounded in possibility and purpose, challenges are perceived as opportunities for expansion. Mental habits, he said, strengthen with practice. Training the mind to recognize growth within struggle reveals paths where others see barriers.

He emphasized the importance of starting honestly—acknowledging one's current position without judgment and building achievable goals. Each success builds momentum. Supportive environments, both tangible and intangible, further reinforce resilience. Mindset becomes the compass, belief the fuel.

The discussion then turned to resilience across cultures and life stages. Mr. Johnson explained that resilience develops dynamically through lived experiences, upbringing, and cultural context. Those raised amidst scarcity or hardship often develop adaptive coping mechanisms early, while others may cultivate resilience later in life. Neither path is superior—each prepares individuals for different challenges.

Cultural narratives also influence how struggle is perceived. Some cultures normalize hardship as growth, while others prioritize stability and comfort. Life stages further shape resilience: youth carries forward momentum, midlife balances responsibility and change, and later life brings acceptance and wisdom.

He emphasized the importance of pausing when confusion arises. Slowing down allows deeper understanding and reveals resources already present. He shared that clarity—not prediction—is what builds resilience, and that various tools and mirrors in life serve either to support or challenge growth.

When Mr. Chatterjee asked how perceived weaknesses can become strengths, Mr. Johnson explained that transformation begins with awareness and self-regulation. Recognizing a limitation with humility opens the door to growth. He shared examples of individuals who reframed challenges—such as a man who discovered dyslexia later in life and transformed listening into a strength, and a woman who turned impatience into a skill of emotional timing and guidance.

The message was clear: life presents challenges that reflect one's current level of maturity. When embraced consciously, these challenges foster self-mastery. Growth, he concluded, comes through presence, careful steps, and gratitude for every mirror that reveals truth.

As the session ended, Mr. Chatterjee sat quietly, absorbing what had shifted within him. When asked to share a word that captured the experience, he chose "Rewriting." It marked a quiet turning point—not the end of grief, but the beginning of healing.

Summary

This book project is a living invitation to connect, reflect, and truly understand one another. It is built on a simple yet powerful idea: when we communicate from the same starting point, understanding becomes possible. Through practicing communication using the same text, readers and listeners learn that most miscommunication does not arise from conflict, but from different beginnings.

Perspective is shaped by experience, access, and literacy. An illiterate person naturally views the world differently from a literate one, not because of lesser intelligence, but because reading and writing nurture the logical and reflective parts of the brain. When literacy grows, so does the ability to reason, articulate, and engage in meaningful dialogue.

This project bridges these differences by offering the content in both reading and listening formats, ensuring that everyone—regardless of background—can begin from the same foundation. From this shared starting point, individuals are encouraged to express, share, and refine their perspectives. Through podcasting, these voices are carried further, allowing personal insights to be heard by many and creating a ripple of collective learning.

The initiative includes two thoughtfully designed books: one for young people and adults, and another for caretakers, recognizing the unique roles each plays in shaping lives and communities.

This is a global initiative, rooted in cooperation and shared purpose. Antar Anger is not a single person—it is teamwork in action, a collective effort driven by collaboration rather than individuality. As part of its global journey, the project will be showcased at the largest book fair in Asia, in Delhi in 2025, where the author will be personally present, engaging with readers, listeners, and collaborators from around the world.

This project is more than a book—it is a movement toward conscious communication, shared understanding, and collective growth

Verses Kindler Publication

Verses Kindler Publication

Reach us through our website -

https://www.verseskindlerpublication.com/

For more information visit our

Instagram or Facebook page.

9 789347 494062

Printed at Repro India Ltd.